DRAFT HORSES

BY
JEROLYN ANN NENTL

EDITED BY
DR. HOWARD SCHROEDER
Professor In Reading and Language Arts
Dept. of Elementary Education
Mankato State University

DESIGNED & PRODUCED BY
BAKER STREET PRODUCTIONS
MANKATO, MINNESOTA

COVER GRAPHICS BY
BOB WILLIAMS

CRESTWOOD HOUSE
Mankato, Minnesota

LIBRARY OF CONGRESS CATALOGING IN PUBLICATION DATA

Nentl, Jerolyn Ann.
  Draft horses.

  (Horses, pasture to paddock)
  SUMMARY: A historical view of the huge, strong animals which are man-kind's work horses, discussing the five main breeds, and how to use and care for them.
  1. Draft horses--Juvenile literature. (1. Draft horses. 2. Horses.) I. Schroeder, Howard. II. Title. III. Series.
  SF311.N43   1983   636.1'5   83-7831
  ISBN 0-89686-233-X

International Standard Book Numbers:
Library Binding 0-89686-233-X

Library of Congress Catalog Card Number:
83-7831

PHOTOGRAPH CREDITS

Pennington Galleries: Cover, 14
Alix Coleman: 4, 16, 18, 38, 45
State Historical Society of Wisconsin: 9
John Cross: 11, 21, 31
Bob Williams: 13, 22, 24, 28-29, 36, 40
Patti Mack: 26, 35
Joseph Berke/Hammitt's Belgians: 33, 42

CRESTWOOD HOUSE
Hwy. 66 South, Box 3427
Mankato, MN 56002-3427

TABLE
OF
CONTENTS

A mixed breed, or "grade," draft horse.

INTRODUCTION

"Look at that!" Marty yelled as he pointed out the car window.

"I haven't seen that in years," his father said, as he slowed the car.

There in the field along the side of the road were eight huge horses pulling a plow. They were hitched together in two teams of four, one team behind the other. The teamster sat high above the plow in a metal seat.

"Let's drive over there and see if we can get a closer look," Marty's father said. "I used to watch your grandfather drive bunch teams like that when I was growing up on the farm."

They turned off the highway onto a gravel road and headed toward the horses. The teamster had just made a wide U-turn and was slowly coming back up the field. As Marty and his father drove up, the teamster stopped the horses, jumped down off the plow, and was walking toward some barrels near the fence.

"Hi," shouted the teamster. "I was just about to get some water for the team." As the teamster got closer to him, Marty saw that it was a woman.

"How can you drive those horses?" Marty asked. Then he added, rather quietly, "I didn't know you were a woman when I saw you from the highway."

The teamster laughed. "My name is Ellen. I can

drive a team because I had a good teacher and I've had lots of practice. I've lived on this farm since I was a little girl, and I grew up around horses. My father taught me. He's retired now, but he's teaching my husband, too, so we can take over the farm."

"I wish I knew how to drive a team of horses," Marty said.

"I'll tell you what we'll do," his father said, putting an arm around Marty's shoulders. "There's a draft horse show at the state fairgrounds this weekend. We'll go so you can see what these gentle giants can really do."

"Good. We'll be there, too," Ellen said to Marty. "I'll introduce you to my father. Maybe he will show you how to harness a horse and hitch up a team."

①
DRAFT HORSES
IN HISTORY

These huge, strong animals are draft horses. They are the work horses of history. No one knows exactly when or where wild horses were first tamed to work. We do know that people were using the horse long before history was ever recorded.

Most work horses are very large. They have been bred for great size and strength. Their ancestors are the wild horses that roamed throughout the continents of Europe and Asia thousands of years ago. These herds of wild horses settled into different parts of the world. This caused them to grow in different ways. Exactly how they grew depended on where they lived and the food they ate. Those that settled in the warmer, southern part of Asia grew to be light, fast and high-spirited in disposition, or nature. Today, these horses are called Arabians. Those that settled in the colder, northern parts of Europe grew to be huge and heavy, slow and calm in disposition. These heavy horses that lived in an area along the North Sea, known as Flanders, were called the Flemish Horse. From these horses came all the heavy horse breeds known today.

WAR HORSES

The huge, heavy horses were first used as war horses during the Middle Ages. This was the time of

Huge horses were used in wars during the Middle Ages.

7

Metal armour weighed hundreds of pounds.

the knights in armor. The armor was made of metal. Sometimes it weighed as much as four hundred pounds (181 kg). The knights needed strong horses that could carry such a load for a long time and still have enough energy to charge into battle. This horse became known as the Great Horse of Europe.

Then gunpowder was invented. The knights, with their heavy armor, were no longer needed. The heavy horses were no longer needed either. Their great strength and endurance, and their calm disposition, did not go to waste, however. They were put into harness to work in the fields and on the streets and roads.

HORSES AS POWER

A padded, pear-shaped horse collar allowed the heavy horse to throw its great strength into pulling a load. An iron horseshoe protected its hoofs from quickly wearing down on paved roads. With "shoes" and a collar the horse could pull very heavy loads over great distances.

The work horse in harness became a common sight in Europe. Some were hitched to plows and put to work on the farms. Some hauled carts and wagons filled with all kinds of goods for sale or trade in the cities. Others pulled buggies and coaches filled with people going from one place to another. Work horses were brought by settlers to North America, too.

A dapple-gray team pulls an early grain wagon in Wisconsin.

No special breeds had been established yet. These were plain, heavy horses. People saw that some horses were better suited than others for certain kinds of work. They began trying to breed horses with certain qualities needed for heavy work. This type of breeding enriched the basic shape, size, speed, and disposition of the heavy work horse. Later, breeders started registration, or stud books. Only the names and ancestors of purebred horses could be recorded in these books.

REPLACED BY MOTOR VEHICLES

The horse was the main source of power until the invention of the engine. The steam engine was invented first. Then came the gasoline engine. With these engines came cars, trucks, buses and trains. Motor vehicles began to haul goods and people across the land. In the fields, farmers were urged to trade in their horses for tractors.

In 1907 there were about six hundred tractors being used in the United States. By 1920 the number of tractors had increased to nearly 250,000. That number increased to 1,500,000 by 1940. It increased to nearly 3,500,000 by 1950.

The number of horses being used on American farms decreased as the number of tractors increased.

During the early 1900's some farms used both horses and tractors. The same thing is happening again today.

By 1918 there were about twenty-seven million work horses. By 1960 there were only three million. No one knows how many there are today. The United States took its last annual farm horse count in 1960.

Cars and trucks have replaced horses in the cities. Trains, planes, and buses help move people from one place to another. Like the tractor, they get the job done faster than horses.

The use of horses as a source of power reached a low point during the 1960's. Work horses seemed doomed to live out their days in pastures or as tourist attractions. Now, in the 1980's, there is a new interest in horse power! Once again these great horses are in demand. They are being used to work small farms and to carry goods in carriages, carts and wagons.

②
THE DRAFT
HORSE BREEDS

Today, there are five main draft horse breeds — Belgian, Clydesdale, Percheron, Shire, and Suffolk. Each breed has its own special qualities and abilities. What they all have in common is their great size and strength. Each stands about sixteen hands high and weighs about one ton (.91 MT). Yet all are calm horses with mild natures. This is why they have earned the name, "gentle giants."

BELGIAN

There are more Belgian horses in America today than all the other four draft horse breeds combined. It is the most direct descendent of the huge Flemish Horse, probably because its ancestors had the same homeland. The Belgian came from the country of Belgium, in the area that used to be called Flanders. Work horses have been bred in Belgium for centuries. The government of that country helps breeders maintain the purity of their breeds and awards prizes for show winners. The Belgian stud book was started in 1866.

Also in 1866, Belgians were brought to the United States for the first time, by Dr. A.G. Van Hoorebeck of Monmouth, Illinois. More were imported in 1885 and 1886 by the Wabash Importing Company of Indiana. The American stud book was started the next year, in 1887. The breed did not increase too much until 1903, however. In that year the government of Belgium showed some of their prize horses at the St. Louis World's Fair. After that display, the number of Belgians in the United States increased quickly.

Americans began to breed the Belgian to suit the country's farmers. The result was a large, powerful horse called the American Belgian. It is now considered by some people to be a separate breed from the Belgian bred in Belgium.

The American Belgian stands sixteen to seventeen

The Belgian is a patient, willing worker.

hands tall and weighs 1,800 to 2,000 pounds (815-905 kg). Most are a reddish-brown chestnut color, called sorrel, with some white markings. The Belgian is a very patient horse and a very willing worker.

CLYDESDALE

The Clydesdale is perhaps the best-known of the draft horses in North America. Their high-stepping, flashy footwork makes them popular at parades and shows. They are often seen pulling large wagons in advertisements.

Clydesdales are often seen in parades. Notice the "feather" on their feet.

These horses came from Lanarkshire, Scotland. Their history is not as well known as that of the Belgian. It is known that they were bred by farmers in the valley of the River Clyde. They were also used to haul coal from the local coalfields. The Clydesdale stud book was started in 1877.

The Clydesdale is not as large as the Belgian. As a rule it stands about sixteen hands high and weighs 1,700 to 1,900 pounds (770-860 kg). Bay and brown are the most common colors, although chestnut and black are also seen at times. All Clydesdales have white markings about the face and lower legs. They also have long, fine leg hairs, called "feather."

The Clydesdale does not have as wide and compact a body as some of the other draft horse breeds. It is often described as "rangy." It has a broad, straight face and a long, arched neck.

The Clydesdale was first imported to North America in the late 1870's. It went to work in America's cities pulling merchants' wagons. The Clydesdale was never as popular with farmers as some of the other draft horse breeds. The reason may have been its flowing feather. Feather and high-stepping action may look good on city streets. On the farm, feather takes a lot of extra care after a hard day's work in a dirty field.

Easy handling, flashy foot action, and feather are the special traits of the Clydesdale.

Percherons have an elegant beauty.

PERCHERON

The Percheron is the only one of the draft horse breeds to have a bit of Arabian horse blood in it. At least that is what some breed experts believe. The head of the Percheron has an elegant beauty that is different from the other draft horse breeds. It is the second most popular draft horse in America, today.

A tiny district of France called La Perche is the Percheron's original home. It is in the Province of Normandy. The area is known for its top-quality horses — both light riding horses as well as heavy work horses. The true beginnings of the Percheron breed are not known. It is believed that local farmers imported Flemish stallions to breed with some of their native mares. They were also bred to pull the huge, heavy coaches of France's kings and queens. Later, they pulled mail and passenger coaches. A Percheron stud book was not started in France until 1885. Only Percherons, born within the tiny district of La Perche, can be recorded in this stud book!

The Percheron was one of the first draft horses imported to North America. Edward Harris of Morristown, New Jersey, imported the first ones in 1839. He had seen these huge horses for the first time while traveling in France. Not many other Percherons followed until the 1850's. For many years after that, however, they were the most popular draft horse in the United States. Its willingness to work found the Percheron a home on many farms. The elegant style of its head and its even gait also found it much work as a coach horse in towns. A stud book was started in the United States in 1876.

Percherons are black or gray. The gray ones turn white as they get older. Often the gray Percherons are dappled, or spotted. Percherons stand up to seventeen hands and weigh 1,900 to 2,100 pounds (860-955 kg). This large size is well-arranged on a firm, strong body. They are noted for extra heavy muscles in their thighs. In action, the Percheron has a high step much like the Clydesdale.

The Shire is the largest draft horse breed.

SHIRE

The Shire is the largest of the draft horse breeds. These horses often stand more than seventeen hands and weigh about 2,200 pounds (1000 kg).

The origin of this breed is not fully known. Experts who breed horses believe the Shire came out of the marshy farmland of eastern England called the Fen land. Its ancestors were the Great Horses of Europe. These horses had been brought across the English Channel to breed with native mares in the middle of the eleventh century. This breeding led to the Old English Black Horse, which came to be known as the Shire. English breeders of the Shire started their stud book in 1878.

The Shire was first brought to the United States in the late 1800's. At first, it was not as well accepted as some of the other draft breeds. One reason may have been the feather it has on its legs, like the Clydesdale. American breeders started their stud book in 1885.

The Shire has immense power. Its forequarters are firm and well-muscled, and its hindquarters are thick and powerful. The Shire's body is wide, deep, and long. There are bay, brown, gray and chestnut-colored Shires, but the preferred color now is black. Four white "socks" and a white face are also sometimes seen on a Shire.

SUFFOLK

The Suffolk is the only draft horse developed just for farm work. It also is the only breed that is always the same color. All Suffolks are chestnut-colored. The color may vary in shade from very dark, liver-colored to very light, sorrel-colored chestnut. Suffolks may also have some white markings.

The smallest of the draft horse breeds, the Suffolk stands fifteen to sixteen hands and weighs 1,600 to 1,800 pounds (725-820 kg). It has a very compact round body, with a short, thick neck and short legs. Its head is long.

The Suffolk also came from England. Farmers of Suffolk and Norwich counties bred these horses to till their lands. Their breeding brought out strength and endurance. English breeders started the Suffolk stud book in 1880.

The Suffolk has great pulling power and is known for the quality called "heart" — it won't give up until a job is done.

There are fewer Suffolks in this country than any of the draft horse breeds. They were first brought to the United States in the 1880's.

UTILITY HORSES

Not all working horses are registered purebreds whose ancestors have their names recorded in a stud book. In the past, proper paperwork was not kept up on many breeds. There are many crossbreeds, too. These are horses with a mixture of the draft horse breeds in them. Purebreds have also been crossed with unregistered stock. This helps improve qualities such as strength and disposition. These are called utility horses, or "grade" draft horses. It does not mean that they are not good horses, because they are not purebreds. Many grade horses are good-looking and strong. They have calm natures and a lot of heart. They have worked in harness for centuries and continue to do so today.

Light riding horses can also be worked in harness, if trained and given proper care. Most of the draft breeds are better at pulling, however, because of their size, shape, and disposition. They are also able to do more work and are easier to handle.

These "grade" horses are part Belgian, and are being used today on a Minnesota farm.

③
RIGGING AND DRIVING THE DRAFT HORSE

To rig a horse means to harness it. There are many different ways to do this. The way that is used will depend on the job to be done and the number of horses to be used. Rigging always includes a harness, bridle, and hitch assembly. A teamster uses the bridle to control and direct the horse. The harness allows the horse to pull and back a load. The hitch assembly connects the horse to the load.

HARNESS

The harness includes the horse collar, the hames, and the traces. Traces are sometimes called tugs.

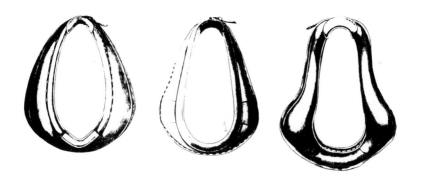

The types of collars: (left to right) full face, half sweeny, and full sweeny.

There are different sizes and shapes of horse collars, but all of them are padded. As a rule, they are made of good leather. The collar fits around the horse's neck. The widest part should always be at the horse's shoulder. This is called the point of draft. All the pressure of pulling a load is at this draft point. That is why working horses are called draft horses.

It is very important that a collar be fitted properly to a horse. Each horse should have its own collar. Collars should be kept in good condition at all times. Anything less than proper fit and good condition could hurt a horse's neck and shoulders.

The hames are two wood or metal pieces that fit into the groove on the outside edge of the horse collar. They are held tightly to the collar by leather hame straps. Each one must be fitted so it is level with the other. On the lower part of each hame is a hook or bolt. These hooks or bolts must be at the point of draft. Therefore, it is important that the correct size hames be used with each horse collar.

The traces, or tugs, are the leather straps, chains or ropes that connect to the hitch assembly so the load can be pulled. They fit into the hooks or bolts on the hames at the point of draft.

Also connected to the harness are many other leather straps, lines, and bands. The most important are the back pad, belly band, breast strap and brichen. The back pad fits across the horse's withers. It helps support the weight of the traces. Sometimes

This photo shows the harnesses in place on a team.

the back pad is called the saddle. The belly band fits underneath the horse, behind its forelegs, and attaches on either side to the traces. It prevents the traces from pushing upwards too far. The breast strap is fastened to the hames and the belly band. The breast band helps the horse to pull its load and to stop. The brichen is the arrangement of leather straps that fits around the rear of the horse, beneath its tail. It fastens through the back pad to the hames. A horse uses the brichen, along with the breast strap, to stop and back its load. Hip drop and back straps hold the brichen in place.

Learning how to properly rig a horse takes a good

teacher and lots of practice. For example, it is very important that the traces fit into the hames at the proper angle. If they do not fit correctly, the collar may be forced against the horse's windpipe. This could choke the horse as it moves forward.

A teamster gets the most strength out of a horse when all parts of the harness are fitted together correctly. A good fit also makes the horse's job easier.

Teamsters know that a work horse is not really pulling a load at all. It is pushing its weight and strength against the horse collar. It is this pushing action that pulls the load. A working horse uses its hindlegs for traction when it pushes into the horse collar. Its forelegs are used for balance.

BRIDLE

The bridle for a work horse is much the same as the bridles used on riding horses. It is an arrangement of leather straps that holds a bit in the horse's mouth. It also supports the reins, called driving lines. The teamster controls and directs the horse by keeping just the right amount of tension on the driving lines.

There are many different kinds of bits. All of them are made of metal. They can be flat, round, twisted or jointed. No matter what the size or shape, each fits

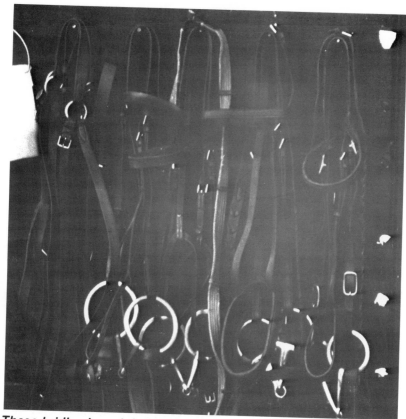

These bridles have jointed bits.

into the horse's mouth. The horse's mouth is very sensitive to any bit. A good teamster remembers this and uses a firm but gentle hand on the driving lines.

Some teamsters like to add blinders (also called blinkers) to their horse's bridle. These are leather pieces attached on either side, next to the eyes. They stop the horse from looking anywhere but straight ahead.

HITCH ASSEMBLY

Work horses can be used alone or hitched together in teams. Two horses may be hitched abreast (side-by-side), or in-tandem (one in front of the other). In-tandem hitches are rarely used for work in North America, but are seen in horse shows and parades. One reason may be because it is a difficult hitch to drive.

Horses also can be hitched together into larger teams. These are called multiple hitches. If more than two pairs of horses are hitched in-line, teamsters call it a string team. The team of horses nearest the teamster is called the wheel team. The team at the front is called the lead team. Each team in between is called a swing team. Teamsters number them, beginning with the first team ahead of the wheel team. They are called first swing team, second swing team, and so on.

If more than two horses are used abreast, teamsters call it a bunch team.

Some of the common multiple hitches are four-up, six-up, eight-up, and nine-up. Four-up hitches have two teams of two horses each. Six-up hitches have two teams of three horses each, or three teams of two horses each. Eight-up hitches have two teams of four horses each, or four teams of two horses each. Nine-up hitches have three teams of three horses each.

Two other types of multiple hitches are the uni-

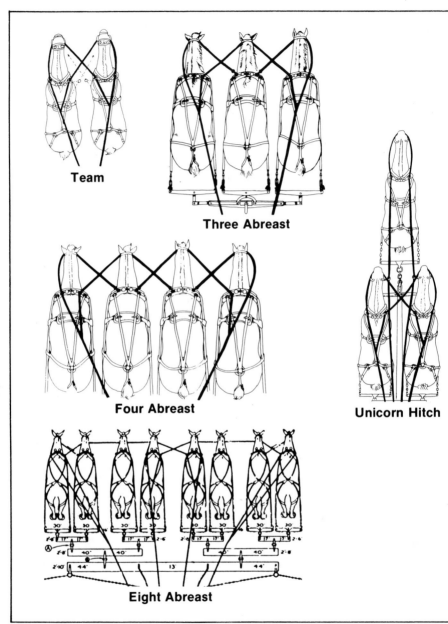

Team

Three Abreast

Four Abreast

Unicorn Hitch

Eight Abreast

Some of the hitches that are used on draft horses.

28

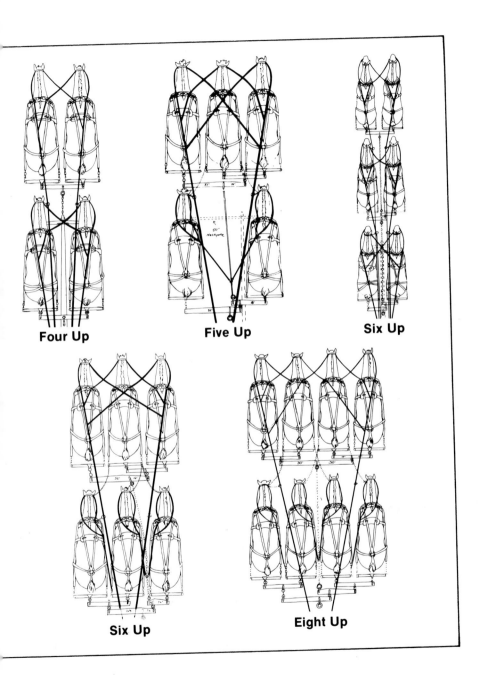

Four Up

Five Up

Six Up

Six Up

Eight Up

29

corn and five-up. The unicorn hitch uses three horses, two behind and one ahead. The five-up hitch uses two horses behind and three ahead.

Each hitch needs a different hitch assembly — neck yokes, singletrees, doubletrees, shafts, tongues, and evener bars. Each hitch also needs a different set-up of driving lines. The number of lines, the length of the lines, and how they will be set up depends on the number of horses.

It takes a very skilled teamster to properly hitch the larger teams. The horses used in these teams must be well-trained, too. With proper training and rigging, the big teams can be driven as easily as a two-horse team!

THE TEAMSTER

Teamsters control their horses with driving lines and word commands.

The driving lines are held in both hands. Left lines rest in the left hand. Right lines rest in the right hand. The teamster applies pressure to the bit in the horse's mouth by pulling on the lines. This is what controls and guides the horse. The lines must never be too loose and never too tight, but just right. This is what is called tension. Proper tension allows the best possible control of the horse without hurting its mouth.

To turn right, a teamster pulls in a small amount

of the right line and lets out an equal amount of the left line. To turn left, the left line is pulled in and the right line is let out. To stop, both lines are pulled in an equal amount. They are released as soon as the horses slow. If both lines are not released, the horses will begin to move backwards.

These line signals should be given at the same time that word commands are spoken to the horses. The basic commands are "get-up" and "whoa" which mean "go forward" and "stop." "Gee" means "go right" and "haw" means "go left." Many horses will also have learned the command "back."

Driving may sound easy, but it is a skill that is learned only after many years of working with horses. It is such a fine skill that driving is sometime considered to be an art. The best way to learn is to find a good teacher and be willing to practice. Learn-

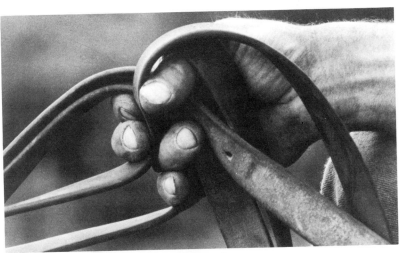

A teamster holds the reins for four horses.

ing is easier if it is done in steps. Beginners do best if they learn how to drive one horse first, then two. After they have mastered driving a pair, they can learn how to drive the larger teams.

TRAINING A HORSE

Training a horse to work in harness should be done only by skilled teamsters. A horse has a short attention span, so training is done in short lessons. Teaching it to accept the bridle and harness is the first lesson. Once it will walk calmly in harness, it can be taught how to accept direction from someone behind it. As a rule, this is done with the teamster walking behind the horse. Only after a horse has learned these two lessons should it be hitched to a load. Learning to pull is done in steps, too. A horse learns to pull light loads first. After it becomes comfortable pulling a light weight, the loads can be made heavier.

A teamster rewards a horse that has done a good job by praising and petting it. Some teamsters like to give their horses a treat, such as a carrot, an apple or a sugar cube.

Horses are smart, feeling animals with good memories. They respond to good care and praise. They will work for the people they respect and trust. Talking to them calmly, using their names, and

Bonds grow when the horse is given good care and respect by the teamster.

33

stroking them gently does much to build these bonds.

④
CARING FOR
THE DRAFT HORSE

All animals need proper care to grow, stay healthy, and live their full lifetime. Proper care is very important for draft horses. Teamsters get the most work out of their horses when they care for them properly. If they are neglected, work horses can become sickly. Sick horses are the ones that get hurt most often, too.

Every horse needs food, water, and a place to live. It also needs to be groomed regularly. How much of each a draft horse needs changes from time to time. It will change according to the kind of work a horse is doing and how often it is working.

A PLACE TO LIVE

Work horses do not need big, beautiful barns. A horse is much healthier and happier in a good pasture.

A good pasture will have plenty of grass and a sturdy fence. It will also have an open shelter and plenty of fresh water.

Each horse needs about two or three acres (about one hectare) of pasture. The fence should be high enough so that no horse can jump over it and strong enough to keep the horses in the pasture. Both wood and wire fences are used for horse pastures.

A three-sided shelter allows horses to get out of the wind and rain. It also protects them from the heat and cold. A horse that has such an open shelter will use less energy to cool and warm its body. It will have more energy left for a good day's work.

A pasture is an ideal area for the draft horse.

Exercising in a paddock is necessary if there is no pasture.

A stable or barn is needed, but it does not have to be fancy. It should be big enough to store all the harnesses, hitch gear, feed, and other equipment. It should also have tie stalls. These are open stalls where a horse can be kept for a short time. Full stalls will also be needed when caring for a sick horse or when a mare is giving birth to a foal. Full stalls are closed on all four sides. Teamsters can feed, water and groom their horses in either tie stalls or full stalls.

The building should have a high ceiling and wide doors so a horse cannot hurt itself. It should also have plenty of light and fresh air, and be easy to keep clean and dry. It helps if the building is next to the pasture. All of these things will make it easier to care for the horses. They will also help the horses stay healthy.

If there is not enough good pasture, the horses must be housed in a barn or stable. Each horse should have its own full stall. The stall can be either a box stall about twelve feet square (3.6 x 3.6 m), or a standing stall that is at least five feet by nine feet (1.5 x 2.7 m).

FEEDING

Just as all engines need fuel to produce energy, a horse also needs fuel for energy. A horse's fuel is food and water. Each horse needs a different amount depending on its size, health, and the amount of work it is doing. The weather may also affect how much food and water a horse needs.

Horses must be fed several times a day. This is because they have small stomachs, for their large size. Their bodies cannot handle a lot of food all at once. As a rule, teamsters feed their horses three times a day — in the morning, during the mid-day break from work, and in the evening after the work day is done.

Grass is a horse's natural food. This is why it is important to have a pasture with lots of good grass.

A Clydesdale mare and her foal share some grain.

If there is not enough grass, or if horses are kept in a barn, they are fed hay. Hay is dried grass. Working horses also need grain. Oats is used most often. Barley, wheat, corn and rye are also good, and sometimes a mixture of grains is used. A horse working a full eight-hour day is fed about one pound (.45 kg) of grain and one to one-and-a-half pounds (.45-.7 kg) of hay for each one hundred pounds (45.5 kg) of its weight each day! Those doing less than a full-day's work will need less feed. Grass or hay (without grain) may provide enough energy on days when the horses are not working.

Along with food, every horse needs plenty of fresh water. A horse may drink twelve to fifteen gallons

(43.7-54 l) of water a day! No horse should ever be allowed to drink a lot of water when it is hot and sweaty. A hot and sweaty horse that drinks a lot of water can get sick. The horse can be given a small amount of water, but then it should be walked and cooled down. After it is cool, it can be allowed to drink freely. A wise teamster allows each horse to drink a small amount of water every few hours while working, especially on hot days. A working horse loses a lot of water from its body when it sweats. This water must be replaced for a horse to stay healthy.

Horses also need salt to stay in good health. Some teamsters mix loose salt with the grain they feed their horses. Others prefer to leave a block of salt where their horses can lick it. Most horses need one or two ounces of salt a day. Working horses may need more than this, because salt is lost when they sweat.

GROOMING

Stabled work horses must be groomed daily. It helps keep a horse healthy. Combs and brushes are used to remove the waste materials a horse gives off through the pores of its skin when it sweats. Grooming also removes mud, dirt, and loose hair.

Horses living out in a pasture need less grooming, but they should have a good brushing before being harnessed. A horse living outside grooms itself natu-

A horse can help groom itself by rolling on the ground.

rally by rolling on the ground, and rubbing against trees and other objects.

As a rule, grooming is done with a currycomb, stiff body brushes, soft face and leg brushes, and clean cloths.

Grooming gives a horse soft skin and a rich, glossy coat of hair. A horse that has rough, dry skin and a dull, dry coat is not being cared for properly.

It is important to pay special attention to a working horse's neck, shoulders and feet. Dirt and loose hair left beneath the horse collar can cause bruises, aches and pains. They may also cause raw sores, called galls.

A horse's hoofs must be cleaned every day with a hoof pick. They may have picked up dirt clods, stones or other objects. These could cause the horse to go lame if they are not removed.

Horses working on rough ground, stones, or paved streets and roads are usually fitted with horseshoes. These are U-shaped pieces of metal fitted on the bottom of each hoof. They prevent the hoof from wearing down too quickly. Horseshoes must be removed every four to six weeks so that each hoof can be trimmed. This is because a horse's hoof grows about one-quarter inch each month. Horseshoes can be reset several times, before new ones must be fitted.

Generally, farm horses working on soft ground do not need horseshoes. Their hoofs must be trimmed regularly, however.

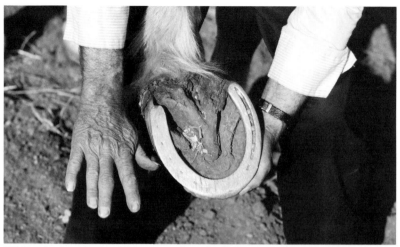

This photo shows the size of a draft horse's foot compared to a man's hand.

Horseshoes may be fitted by a farrier, but many teamsters know how to shoe their own horses.

OTHER CHORES

Teamsters must also take good care of their harness and hitch gear. Leather pieces, such as the collar and straps, have to be kept clean and oiled so they do not become hard and brittle. Wood and metal pieces must also be kept in good repair. If they are not cared for, they could break and hurt a horse or a teamster. Such a mishap could cause a horse to bolt and run away. A run-away horse is a danger to itself, other horses in a team, and to the teamster!

Good teamsters understand the needs of their horses and are concerned about their well-being.

They never ask them to do more work than they are able to do. They never ask them to work when they are sick or hurt. Good teamsters are willing to spend the time and effort necessary to properly care for their horses.

⑤
THE VALUE OF DRAFT HORSES

Many people like working with horses because they are living, feeling animals instead of machines. Together they can build a bond of trust, respect, and understanding that make them true partners in work. A good teamster can get a horse to go where no machine could go, and do what no machines could do.

In the past they were used to pull a wagon out of the mud, or to pull a heavy load up a very steep hill. Horses did these jobs easily for hundreds of years. The jobs are different in the modern world. Today, cable may have to be strung across a deep ravine. Pipeline may have to be laid through a frozen land. These are jobs that draft horses can handle.

Many qualities make the work horse valuable today, just as in years past. Perhaps most important of all, are the many different ways in which horses can work. A horse can be used alone. It can be used with farm implements such as the plow. It can be used with vehicles such as a wagon or carriage.

Teams can be hitched together for more power and strength. The only real limit is the imagination and know-how of the teamster and the number of horses available. Forty horses have been hitched together and driven!

Work horses are valuable for other reasons, too. Horses are good to the earth. Their hoofs do not compact the soil, like heavy machines do. Horses use homegrown fuel — hay and grain. The fuel they use is returned to the earth in the form of manure. This helps enrich the soil. Unlike machines, horses are a power source that renews itself. A horse may work for up to twenty years, leaving behind many offspring. These new horses may work for another twenty years each. Foals produced by working mares can be sold, if teamsters do not want to add to their own work stock. As a rule, horses are self-repairing, unlike machines. No spare parts are needed, although teamsters must care for their partners in work to keep them strong and healthy. Horses are not as expensive to buy as machinery, either. A work horse may cost nothing, if a foal has been born.

THE DRAFT HORSE REVIVAL

Most people consider draft horses a thing of the past. But there are still a few people around, young and old, who love these big animals and believe in them. Their numbers, and the number of draft horses in North America, are increasing for the first time in twenty years.

Draft horses are not for everyone. Driving them is a real challenge. It is for people who are tired of the fast pace of the world today and want to slow down. These people want to get away from machines and the pollution they can cause. They want to get closer to the earth, and warm, friendly animals. For these people, driving horses can be soothing and refreshing.

Horses will never replace tractors, trucks, and all the other kinds of modern machines. But the people who breed and drive the "gentle giants" are helping these huge draft horses take their rightful place in today's modern world.

A pair of "gentle giants."

GLOSSARY

ABREAST - Two or more horses hitched side-by-side.

ACTION - A horse's way of moving its feet.

BRIDLE - The arrangement of straps used to control and direct draft horses; made up of the head-piece, bit and driving lines.

BUNCH TEAM - A multiple hitch team with more than two horses used abreast.

DRIVING LINES - The leather straps used by the teamster to control and direct the horses; the driving lines connect to the bit in the horse's mouth.

FARRIER - A person that puts on horseshoes.

FEATHER - The long, fine hairs on the legs of some breeds of draft horses.

FLEMISH HORSE - An ancient heavy horse from northern Europe; all of today's draft horse breeds are descended from this horse.

GRADE DRAFT HORSE - Draft horse of no special breed.

GREAT HORSE - The horse used to carry knights in armor during the Middle Ages; descended from the Flemish Horse, and is an ancestor of all of today's draft horse breeds.

HAND - The measurement used to measure the height of a horse from the ground to its withers. A hand is equal to four inches (10.3 cm).

HAW - A command that tells a horse to turn left.

HITCH ASSEMBLY - The arrangement of wood

and metal pieces, leather straps, and chains that connects the harness to the load.

IN-TANDEM - Horses or teams hitched one in front of the other.

LEAD TEAM - The team of horses at the front of the hitch, farthest from the teamster.

MULTIPLE HITCH - More than one pair of horses used together.

POINT OF DRAFT - The widest point of a horse collar which must fit exactly on a horse's shoulder; all the pressure of pulling a load is at this point.

PUREBRED - A horse whose ancestors have all belonged to one special breed.

RIGGING - The equipment used for working horses; rigging includes the harness, bridle and hitch assembly.

STRING TEAM - A multiple-hitch team with three or more pairs of horses hitched in-line.

SWING TEAM - Each team of horses in between the lead team and the wheel team.

TEAM - Two or more horses hitched together for more pulling power.

TRACES - The straps, chains, and ropes that connect the harness to the hitch assembly.

WHEEL TEAM - The team of horses nearest the teamster.

WITHERS - The highest point on the shoulder of a horse.

WHOA - A command that tells a horse to stop.

THE HORSES
PASTURE TO PADDOCK

**READ & ENJOY
THE ENTIRE SERIES:**

CRESTWOOD HOUSE

DATE DUE